BY BRACKFIELD BAWN

On Being in Brackfield Memorial Woods

Sam Burnside

With a Foreword by Helen Mark

❖

❖

Belfast
LAPWING

First Published by Lapwing Publications
c/o 1, Ballysillan Drive
Belfast BT14 8HQ
lapwing.poetry@ntlworld.com
http://www.lapwingpoetry.com

British Library Cataloguing in Publication Data.
A catalogue record for this book is available from
the British Library.

Since before 1632
the Greig sept of the MacGregor Clan
has been printing and binding books

Lapwing Publications are printed and
hand-bound in Belfast at the Winepress.
Set in Aldine 721 BT

ISBN 978-1-910855-63-8

BY THE SAME AUTHOR

Poems

The Cathedral, Freehold Press, Belfast, 1989.
Walking the Marches, Salmon Poetry, Galway, 1990.
Horses, limited edition handmade book with original wood engravings by Tim Stampton, Ballagh Studio, Co. Donegal, 1993.
Fahan Mura, with an introduction by Frank Harvey, Lapwing Publications, 1995.
A Will to Remember, with an introduction by Kerry Hardie, Linen Hall Library, Belfast, 2003.
Innocents Abroad, with a foreword by Frank McGuinness, Arttank Gallery, Belfast, 2004.
New and Selected Poems, UHF, Belfast, 2013. (www.booksireland.org.uk)
Forms of Freedom, with an introduction by John Gray, Lapwing Publications, Belfast, 2015.

For Children

A Story of Mice, Verbal Arts Centre, Londonderry, 2000.
Mrs Nettlebed's Year, Green Road Press, 2014 (www.booksireland.org.uk).
Mrs Nettlebed and the Woodlanders, Green Road Press, 2015 (www.booksireland.org.uk).

Prose

Writer to Writer, Community Creative Writing, Workers' Educational Association, Belfast, 1990.
Training and Arts Administration in Northern Ireland, Workers' Educational Association, Belfast, 1991.
One Word - Many Roots, Oral Traditions Across the Regions, Verbal Arts Centre, Londonderry, 1995.
The Magic Circle, The Literary Life of a City, Verbal Arts Centre, Londonderry, 2002.
Individuals, Communities and the Notion of Progress, Tim Coates Books, London, 2009.

As Editor

The Glow Upon the Fringe,
Literary Journeys around Derry and the North West,
edited by Sam Burnside, with an introduction by D.E.S. Maxwell,
Verbal Arts Centre, Londonderry, 1994.
Ourselves and Others, Twenty-One Award Winning Poems,
Western Education and Library Board, Omagh, 1988.
Borderlines (A Collection of New Writing from the North-West),
with a preface by Frank McGuinness,
Holiday Projects West, Londonderry, 1988.

ACKNOWLEDGEMENTS

I wish to thank the Woodland Trust, and the Trust's Brackfield Memorial Woodland Advisory Committee, for their invitation to me to engage with what is a wonderfully simple yet hugely rich experiment in historical remembrance. Namely, the establishment of a woodland dedicated to the 400,000 men and women from this island who participated in the First World War. Of these, 40,000 were not to return. This new planting has been dedicated to their memory.

I want to record here the unanimous and very positive response by all of those who were involved to the proposal that I should explore the woods - and their new-minted significance as a place of island-wide commemoration through the medium of poetry; and then for their decision to make use of a number of these poems in the creation of an innovative poetry trail set in the heart of the memorial woods.

Finally, my thanks to all those who read the poems at an early stage and who made comments and suggestions or who gave advice on matters of fact, especially to Maurice Healy for his, as always, ever-critical reading.

Sam Burnside

CONTENTS

PREFACE

A fragment of family memory came back to me as I was reading *By Brackfield Bawn*. It involved our two boys, both then at primary school, and the old spreading beech tree at the end of the garden. They called it 'The Thinking Tree'. Why such a name? Well, its gnarled roots, breaking proud of the surface made for a snug place to sit in, the smooth trunk a comfortable backboard. I had settled myself there in the dappled light to consider a change in my career. I've always felt grounded and calmed in the company of trees so it felt the right place to be. "What are you doing Mummy?" was their plea. "Thinking!" said I. And so it was forever christened.

A small but precious memory awoken by Sam Burnside's collection of poems which release, re-imagine, relive a multitude of memories, both ancient and modern, that have been stored in this beautiful wooded valley of the River Faughan. His poems are brimming with his knowledge of this place, its history, its people, its changes through time and he helps us visualise Brackfield's significance far beyond its valley limits. He celebrates the natural world especially when it comes to the trees. From the ancient Ardmore Oaks, witness to our distant past, to those in Brackfield Wood still in their infancy - not least the 40,000 planted to pay tribute to those from across the island of Ireland who lost their lives during the First World War. Sam so poignantly instills a century old memory of loss in these young saplings.

From his words you'll know that Sam's been at Brackfield in all weathers, through all seasons and has drawn both inspiration and pure joy from the character and beauty of wood and vale, of the river and wildlife. His deep sense of place for this landscape is palpable and I relish walking in his footsteps with this collection in hand, particularly through Brackfield's trees planted either by our ancestors, or natures hand or by workers or families, be it for remembrance, for fun, for love, in sorrow and loss, for healing or with hope for the future. Between them what an insightful path we can now weave....for that, I thank you Sam.

Helen Mark

Sam Burnside

David Baird, d. 1st July 1916, Somme.

What kind of times are they, when
A talk about trees is almost a crime
Because it implies silence about so many horrors?

Bertolt Brecht

By Brackfield Bawn

HERE

When I hear water
I know I have reached home

When I hear bird-song
I know I am not alone

THE LANTERN

Remember them alive:
Hold up this lantern
Against the dark night.

Remember their lives:
Live your own life
In the light of the sun.

By Brackfield Bawn

BRACKFIELD

Traveller
As you pass by, on your way from Belfast
To Derry, or from Londonderry to Park,
Take a moment to slow down, to pause,
Pull in at the Bawn and stop the engine
And open the door and listen; sounds,
Thrumming all about you.

Over the fields
Lies Claudy, where Simmons, by his song, pinned that day;
Embers from old fires smoulder long and slow.
Beneath your feet, feel deep-dug foundations
Shiver. Gun-slits, opening to field and wood -
They groyne the earth, they tell of fears long nursed:
So, muskets here; there, at Burntollet, stones flying,
With prayers and muttered curses, mingling.
Cross the road to the valley-lip - mark the river,
Trees, hills cascading, clouds, wind in your hair,
The sky above. Conjure up the generals,
Kings, highwaymen, peasants, the planters and the planted,
The Gaels and the Celts, workers from Poland -
Men and women whose presence this ground concedes.

Stand
Let air and sun kiss your skin incarnate.
Acknowledge those who were here, those who conferred
On you this gift of life, left you this heritage
Willed you a choice - peace or war, life or death.

Inhale, breathe out:
Rooted trees, glints of cold running water,
White-tongued, falling - tumbling - over granite:
Take lessons from, cultivate faith in, these:
Root and branch coupled by living wooded bole
Trees make woods and woods make forests complete
In this way, earth and heaven stand united;
Rooted tree and open mind and pumping heart.

Sam Burnside

FALLEN HERO

They were in Iceland when orders came:
They took to the air in darkness, lifting,
Marshalling themselves, arrow-head formatted,
Wings-flapping, whooping, driving forward,
Ploughing the air, neck-pumping, ignoring
Thermals, ignorant of icy depths beneath.

Dawn-pearled heaven's clouds, threading with gossamer
That command, pledging the purpose of their passage:
Their leader fell there, just short of the coastline,
The northern loughs of Ireland within sight
Glinting, blinking in the cold morning light,
Signalling, *Welcome, Welcome. Welcome home.*
Again, and again, *Ye who remain.*

By Brackfield Bawn

KING OF THE WOODS

i

Four ancient oak trees stand, shambled,
Looking down to where the Faughan flows
The King of Trees with his three weird children
Following on; all four gnarled old fork-benders, long
Waiting, derelict as they are, once well-crowned heads
Wispy and devoid of leaf or life
As the other was when another denounced his wife.
They wait here, their great majestic bodies growing crabbed,
Waiting for the Queen of the Woods to come calling,
To come riding by, waving her wand.

ii

Your Majesty:
If I may be so bold
What you need is love
A bit of care and attention
What you need is a massage
To ease the joints of those arthritic old limbs
A hair-do and a pedicure
A manicure and a little oil, rubbed
Patiently into that tired dry crust.
What you lack, my King of Trees, is a little love.

Sam Burnside

THE QUEEN OF THE WOODS

Her head is in the clouds
Her feet planted in the earth
Queen of the Woods
Her crown is a shelter
Her head green-garlanded
A home and a sanctuary:
Her great body is buckled
And twisted; yet, her demeanour
Speaks of old decency.
The Queen and her courtiers
Derelict as they are
Respect ancient royalty:
She remains the Beech Queen
Whose consort is the Oak King.

By Brackfield Bawn

PARADIGM

You dropped a pebble into the shallows
While we watched it fall, barely hearing the plop
(Perhaps we noticed only its falling, imagining more).
After it entered, we saw the first ring form
Then those widening circles, their multiplication.
Somehow, we missed the crux -
That point when the change occurred
And the retreat began - your intercession with nature
Having come to nothing: the radiating ripples
Seemingly mediated by another rhythm,
That of passing horses' hooves - gallop, canter, trot
While horses' tails seemed to sweep the water
So lightly, mixing the glimmer of hawthorn's
New green leaves with big brown, horse chestnut
Buds, fat and tender and splitting wider
And wider; opening, revealing as we looked
An inner life. Then, dandelion-yellow, tingeing all
Pink and purple leaves, verging into greenness.
One pebble - then all this - swirling colours, shades, hues.
Your slight white hand, shimmering.
Such a derangement of nature's palette.

Sam Burnside

BATTLEFIELD

Remembering TP Flanagan

A field of chalk
Chalk-dust brushed
Hoar frosted
Pearly
Pale, but not pallid
A single strand of barbed wire
Running from left to right
Blood and rust tinctured
A few fence posts, warped, moth-eaten
Bleached
Serving little purpose
That, and
Grave markers, and
Blades of green grass -
That is the all of it.

By Brackfield Bawn

BODY ARMOUR

A hedgehog noses blindly,
Without grace, he trundles,
Grunting among tangled grasses.

A soldier steps by, smartly,
All precision and shine,
All boot-spit-and-polish.

The hedgehog halts, tastes danger,
Blind insight, ancient senses trigger
His swift curl into a spiny ball.

The soldier is breast-plated by paper -
This one essay of love his hope, his shield.

Sam Burnside

A SOLDIER'S WAY

The bridge is down, kaput.
A soldier stands on the far bank
I have been from home to hell -
Then, this Eden beckoned ...
Days and nights are speeding past.
The morning dew lies late -
It settled early on shy fern
On reed and rush, on dock and stinging nettle
To his boots, damp, dead leaves cling
Small white, brittle bones splinter beneath his heel
His boots are heavy; his passing unsettles
A musky universe of weighty smells
There may be myrtle here.
Of lavender, I have had more than enough!
Sunlight dapples rough tree bark and the greening lawn
Light-and-shade ebb-and-flow, swallows' shadows
Cross the blue-belled slopes
Somewhere, a keening curlew rises above the dawn
Its swift echoes follow on and on, briefly
The ranked trees exhale; another dawn chorus erupts.
The four winds come to embrace wood and stone
And water and leaf
Out of darkness, the bridge rises once again, incorrupt.

By Brackfield Bawn

DUST

The stonebreaker is all muscle and bone
An old cart axle eaten by rust
He is layered in dust
Stone dust, like a close cap, clings to his shaven skull
And cold peat ash inert on the stone-flanked hearth lies
The air is heavy with spores
Dropped from his thin brother's, the farmer's, duds:
That morning they heard the one dull thud
Barred sunlight fell diagonally, devotionally,
Down and then across the kitchen floor
Draping their mother's bolted bedroom door.
Shrouded there, her thin lips drawn tight in her cell of silence.
The air is all moats and absences.

THE HEDGE BUILDER

Ardlough Road, 23 February 2016
A man I knew said, give me a thorn and I will grow you a forest

That morning, snow had blown in over the Sperrins
Turning northwards, swirling up the Faughan Valley
The hedge-builder was at work
Where the Ardlough Road borders Brackfield Wood.
He worked in sunshine
For now, the snow showers had passed.
It was an alive, sentient early-Spring day –
The swirling snow, the sudden racket of a chainsaw
The flapping blanket of sunshine, the peeling clouds
A clamour of change was in the air
Arms bared to the elbow, he straightened,
Turning away from his willow and ash, to greet me,
Away from his stakes and pleachers, all
Topped with a binding of oak.
He stepped back, inviting me to admire his work.
As he talked, I could see the shadow of his father,
A strong presence over his shoulder.
That man taught me everything, he said.
As I turned away, taking my leave,
He spoke, looking to the hedge,
And do you see that, indicating with a nod of his head.

By Brackfield Bawn

A HEDGE OF HOLLY, THORN AND OAK

A hedge of holly, thorn and oak
A thicket long, broad and tangled
A thing of shelter, a place of rest
A green and black wall with windows small
Dressed in curtains verdant, row on row
And pegs to hang cobwebs; and alleyways
For creatures of the night to go
Or come, and riggings for perches,
With good foundations for nests:
A hedge of holly, thorn and oak.

Sam Burnside

THE TREE BY THE GATE

Winter revealed the pigeon's nest.
In spring, the pair returned
To their carelessly-built saucer-
Shaped bundle of twigs, dropped untidily and left:
I noticed above this, the beginning
Of a different form and weight,
Denser, with roof and entrance,
For by then my magpies had materialised.
All spring I watched them at work
Willing success to their endeavours.
Yet, their reputation hung like a stench in the air:
I might have wrecked the nest, but did not.
Instead, I offered an amnesty,
Sacrificed the pigeons' futures for theirs.
Brackfield set out on loan, they live on scraps;
I observed with pride the offspring that became mine.
So many little harmonies discovered
Through such comings and goings,
Epiphanies birthed, hammered, sparks flying
And caught, emerging marriages of shared existences.
Later, one morning, a cupful, then buckets-full
Of sound deluged down, over my head,
Their young demanding sustenance.
Today, although far from arrogant
(He is merely indifferent to my gaze)
He waits, before dropping
Stone-like behind the thorn hedge
And is gone; yet, I cannot help but feel
I am more than mere spectator: I am
Grateful for those few lent moments.

By Brackfield Bawn

THE FOUR FIELDS OF IRELAND

Much as I should wish it other, there is no thing
Visible under this descending grey sky
That might turn the day celebratory. Then
For a moment, I imagine
A taut rope stretched across the valley's chasm
High above the Faughan's black, cold water
And young man after young man, file on file,
Short and tall, fat and thin, dark and fair,
Marching here from the four great fields of Ireland
Stepping out, arms swinging, boot following boot,
Until the beat of so many feet sets the thin line throbbing
With shared purpose, however distant, and honour,
Shared among so many, however dearly accounted,
Weighed in that forge where fear and pride are smelted.
No matter how many fall, tumbling, head over heel,
Falling in time, falling in time
Another steps forward, the emptiness filled.

ROAMING IN THE BARONY OF TIRKEERAN

As you walk here, pray pay the most careful attention:
Look and see
Read the river, comprehend
The imprint of bugs' feet on the mirrored surface, on
The cheeks on shallows; look, notice the insistences,
Laid on skin of polished cold coal
Glance at rabbit-runs, drawn charcoal-dark on green
Cuckoos and crisp corncrakes rattle through the air.
Study trees, their bark and leaf
Frosted and crimped or wind-blown or dew-damp
Feel the smart of that first raindrop
How it surprises your skin, the stinging sharp imprint,
The sudden coolness in the air
The darkening sky, a cloak descending, lower, lower
Notice cold tree trunks, each with a snow-crusted side,
Under winter sun, sparkling. Scan the sky, the clouds
Their shape and form, their hues
The slowness of them, see and feel
Rain, drizzle, mizzle, water falling like stair rods
Summer showers drifting, passing,
Revealing the glory of rainbows
Dew on grass, on leaf, soft as sweat on a young girl's lip
Read the past, the passage of ice
The marks of man: the felled tree
The ploughman's headland, the fisherman's beat,
Precious stone on stone laid.

By Brackfield Bawn

THE METTLE OF PLACE

The spirit of these
Woods watches
Over
The spotted field
Breacfiadh
Sees
The sunshine
On
The speckled field
Hears
The swift river's
Going
The silver salmon's
Coming
Her black spots
Materialising
While
Traversing
The Faughan
Smolts leaving
The waters
Of the speckled
The spotted
Field
Breacfiadh

Sam Burnside

SALMON SONG

The river ran shimmering and glittering
Then the storm broke, rain spilling

In peaty tears, down from the hills
Water brackish, darkness filled

My skin's eyes know skin, dark and light,
Star-studded, sky bright

Arm in, fully to the oxter,
My wrist intent, my hand a raptor's

My fingertips and his bones meet
His body is neither dry nor moist

His tail shudders, he is gone
The singer following the song

Whispered into fear
He is elsewhere, yet he is here

My finger and his bone are one
As I, the moon and the sun

By Brackfield Bawn

DEEP WATERS

The river water is smooth today
Smooth, but folded in upon itself, two-faced
Fold upon fold, secretly, shiftily,
Swiftly flowing on and on underneath
But to mortal eyes, slow and shallow
Yet, deep and treacherous
Deeper than mere deception need be.

It secretes its treasures in fishy places
It protects its spotted silver and gold
Its black-freckled, finger-printed lovers of chicanery
Bamboozlers amongst flickering shadow and light
Like shades that dance in these their ghostly halls
They partner each other, for misdirection's sake.

Sam Burnside

FIDELITY

Remember
Some leaders, long dead
Took these remembered here and led them.
Think of them and honour well
Each follower's fealty.

Out there,
Beyond the ditch and hedge
The A6 carries lorries
Omnibuses, juggernauts,
Joyous wedding cars and stately hearses.

In here,
Birds are arranging leaves,
Hanging out sheets of music.
Dripping notes off branch and twig,
Harmonies trustingly curling and falling.

By Brackfield Bawn

PAGES

The white bits represent silence
The black - ding dong, ding dong, ding dong

GODSEND

It rained late last night.
Bare branches stand wet and hard against a clear sky.
Gossamer zephyrs (flow-on-flow) pass by.
Excitedly, raindrops dance, mizzling, drizzling, luminous.

OUT ON EXERCISES

Lost in a forest
Of groves
Nowhere to go
Except down cul-de-sacs
Trees everywhere
Panicking in alcoves
Or scratching in corners
Of the mind.

So meagre our merriment
These last days - so little fuss
Merely oppressively darkening days, minds too;
Reek drifting lightly, disturbing what sight
The light of common day might bring.
And us, under this leaking leafy roof,
Making strange with the day and the night
The dimness and the brightness.

By Brackfield Bawn

YAWL

Spring. Another Spring.

Beneath nests we walked
Silent we, silent they
When, from one, a yawling cry came, then
At our feet, the slightest of thuds.

No other sound.

There it lay - evicted, near naked, pulsing
Beneath a coat of greyish down.
We left it, as the books say we should.
And stepping on continued our awkward silent way.

Sam Burnside

MEDITATIONS

On Francis Ledwidge

Heroes

What is it, this delight we have in heroes?
Is he not a brave man who ventures onto quicksand?
Having tuned his ear to the winds blowing
Across Europe, over Ireland?
Who, turning now his eye to the roads ahead,
Steps out, testing each step for the step's sake
A champion over his own fear and foreboding
Alone in a world of storm and earthquake.

Poet of the Blackbird

Turning his back on the rusting plough
His young heart hungry for more
The poet of the blackbird follows the call
From here to there; turning this way, then that:
Others too,
Ireland's men of the soil, leathered hands
Offering up bouquets of primrose and bluebell,
Violet, buttercup and willow herb.

The sheen; the lustre; the wet wood sorrel weeps
Its white flowers close, its heart-shaped leaves fold:
The pity of it, the love of it - until, finally,
Their peasant-poet turned soldier-poet,
Disturbs truth where all truth hides untold,
Deep at the heart of his art.

By Brackfield Bawn

EASTER SONG

On the hillside, a hare leaps
Then another: side by side
They hang, spread-eagled for all time,
Caught between heaven and earth
For all eternity.

In their mock-battle with gravity
Filled with the ebullience of love's passion
They remain, as if nailed to some wooden stake
In the ecstasy that burgeons
When sanity and insanity merge.

Sam Burnside

THE MUSTERING

Clandeboye, 22 April 2016

It is a midday in April, a Spring day, when we arrive.
Three things she asks us to note; meanwhile
The views from the windows are lyrical, pastoral:
The grounds, the trees, the river, turning lake.
Those swans. On that hill, she speaks in welcome, pointing,
You can glimpse Helen's Tower, just a mile away,
Young men - and women - gathered there to be trained,
As soldiers and nurses.
Above lake-water a shard of ice
Shimmers, melting in the heat of the day.
And then that table, the round one in the corner,
That is where we met and sat together
To talk of a coming age, of soil and seed
Disparate people hoping to realise a dream
To dig holes, to plant trees. To not-forget.
She turns away, looking out:
Last autumn we stood here watching a coming generation,
Over there, moving among the fallen fruits;
Gathering, once again.

Three things mentioned; whorled and endless
As a snail's shell, the convoluted affairs of humankind.
High above the lake, a double helix spirals,
Buckling beneath the sun's stern eye.

By Brackfield Bawn

THE AIRMAN AND THE FISH

I went down the hill today
I crossed the field this day
To where the river flows from the hills above Claudy
Tramping through the long grass
Holding in my hand a hazel wand
(Technically, I suppose I had stolen it
As I made my way through the oak wood
As a savage would, I broke it from its tree,
Greedy for its arrowed straightness).
Then here I was thinking of fish
When suddenly
I dreamed; I could be a fisherman
Like that man further along the bank,
His bending rod and barely visible taut line
Not molesting the flowing water at all,
But, nevertheless,
Connecting him to an underwater world
Of fairy lore and dream
The unreality of trout and salmon
Denied to us mere humans.
The river's surface was like a mirror
Reflecting a cloud, a tree, a passing bird,
A donkey ambling along the far bank
Its ghostly image mimicking
All that I till then believed might be real.
I swished my hazel rod through empty air
Just then, the beast groaned,
Grunted unexpectedly -
Just as I was mulling on Yeats, while
Considering my hazel wand,
Unpeeled as it was, and reflecting on my lack of a berry
When, torpedo-like, torpedo-shaped but slender, it was
Lean and trim, beneath the gleam
A form appeared and disappeared

Cloud-like and flimsy, but having body nevertheless, moving
Under, above, sand and gravel
Lighter than cloud, weightier than donkey
Beyond all borders, beyond mind's grasp,
There, gone - leaving only the ghost of this song
On my inner ear.

By Brackfield Bawn

A POEM FOR CHILDREN OF ALL AGES

Come with me when the moon fills the sky
Like a big balloon, butter and milk
And the moth and the bat are on the air
Walk with me by the ponds where fat frogs plop,
Singing, hey-day, hey-day, hey-day-hey
Come down to the river where an ancient salmon waits.

He is the Salmon of Knowledge

Solitary, alone, oddly cold-looking of body, strangely heavy of spirit
His fish soul is thirsty for the hard, glassy water
In that stream set between mountain and sky.

Beware of deep waters!

Stop! Listen to the barking of dogs, cutting through the night
And the far-off buzz of other human children at play
Listen to the sounds of that other country - calling, calling.

Close your ears
Do not listen

Step out with me, beneath this canopy of fireflies
Let us explore the darkness, let us darken our eyes.

Can you not see that fairy ring?
Look! The grass is trodden, flattened...

Imagine,
The fairy girls and boys dancing

I cannot see their faces

Their coats fall open
Gems gleam in the moonlight.

Do not believe your eyes!
Take care! Take care!

Is that not a Mayday pole?
There in that village of foxgloves,
Each petal is home to a small being.

Mischief
Mischief is in the air
Mischief darts about their heads

Do you see that dry leaf rise and fall?
Doff its cap and curtsy, laughing.
Is this not a magic realm?
Can you not feel another world built, dream upon dream?

Fairies and Elves
Do not listen if they call,
Do not follow if they ask
Instead
Hold tight this red round rowan berry
Come home, and there be merry.

By Brackfield Bawn

CARNIVAL NIGHTS

On carnival nights
When the moon is bright
And the fairy rings are full
Then the little folk all
Leap, tumble and fall
On the Oak Woods floor
Laughing, calling for more,
More, the music loud
The sky filled with light
When, look,
Suddenly - a cloud
Thunder and rain falling
It falls in puddles, louder
Each new drop, murdering
The poor moon's pale face.
Plop, plop, plop, they race.
Then, see,
Through briar patch and weed
The startled good folk speed.

SPEAKING OF TREES

I watch our two daughters' five children playing
Tripping through dappling shadows, exploring
Adventuring, calling out, laughter cascading.

Other images resurge; I recall -
Chimneys rising out of low, quiet buildings
Flames spurting, subsiding; ash following, hanging, falling.

Planes pass overhead, wedges of wild geese
Eggs, bombs diarrhoea-skitter the sky, dropping,
Trenches filled with men and mud and broken shells.

We nomadic liberals, we are snared: should we,
Should we not, purge memory for harmony's sake?
I watch, I wonder: should I or not, speak of trees?

I watch our two daughters' five children playing
Among the trees, in dappling shadows exploring
Adventuring, calling out, laughter cascading.

Wedges like lost geese pass overhead.
Bombs drop, like egg-diarrhoea skittering
Over men, heads in trenches, heels in the air
Wedges like lost geese pass overhead.
Bombs drop, like egg-diarrhoea skittering
Over men, heads in trenches, heels in the air

By Brackfield Bawn

BATTLE'S END

Caked mud and dust adorned your boots.
The one place you can be sure of is here
Under this canopy, take off your boots,
Feel the cool grass under your feet, the moss
Swathed softly under your feet, rest,
Stretch out your hand and feel this tree trunk's rough crust
Fret the skin on the palm of your hand.
Ease the wood's foliage around and about your shoulders
Like a blanket, or a shroud,
Mantled so, lie back
Ease yourself into loam,
Leafy and moss soft;
Become a part of it
In a way, you never were part of the race
Or it of you
Sense the wind roaming among treetops before it leaves.
It is time; the ultimate question must be posed - whispered -
Into the silence
And silence is the only answer you will ever get.
Light fades and darkness falls, soft as falling snow.
Ears fill, the nose fills, and the eyes fill, soon
Leaf mould will creep between cold lips,
It will rest there on your stiff, stilled tongue.
You and the earth will be becoming as one,
As one, facing the silent invasion.

FAREWELL TO FAUGHAN

A Lullaby

The light is fading, my child
From far away a voice is calling
The light is fading, my boy
The light is fading, my darling one
Darkness is falling.

I hear the tramp of boots from across the valley.
A heaviness lies on my heart.
The wind has risen. The moon is waxing, now.
On the hawthorn tree, blossoms glow, they dance, as if alive:
Draw the curtain. Draw the curtain close.

The lights are out, my boy,
The lights are out, my only child
My heart is empty of all joy
The lights are out, my poor lost boy.
Darkness has fallen.

By Brackfield Bawn

BUZZARD

Lazy, elliptical, in no hurry, imperial:
I glimpsed the quartering shadow
Of him who has risen from rest: regally,
Handling his reins loosely, so masterful.

I followed darkness as it crossed over
From waltzing on grass to skating on water
I knew then, this was not his shadow
Rather, it was his shadow's reflection, merely that:

An effigy, a likeness, an echo
Of his shadow's shadow
An assassin's emissary grew
Cloaked in a fey and sweaty dew.

HAWK

From behind shuttered eyes he watches,
Then drops; like a stone he falls
And is gone among the rushes.
Between one heartbeat and the next.
His job is done.
He rises, taloned feet clenched.

Sam Burnside

ROOTS OF LIBERTY

Here, buried at noon under shadow
In the place where all shadows meet
Under earth and rock, the shadow's shadow grows
Its brutishly slow progress never complete.

Here, tap-root and hair-root grapple with stony soil.
Feeding for life, living things too shoulder their shapes
Between root and rock into forms long shaped by toil.
Here, sanctuaries of form become anchorages.

By Brackfield Bawn

LOSS

Absence is a measure of silence that exists between two notes,
That stretches out to blistering Mars and galaxies of cold stars.

Absence is that void through which you notice
The purling beck's
Stammering murmur,
The snuffle of leaves, a breath of air kissing your neck.

Absence is the wholeness of silence,
Broken by the comfort found in the bite
Of some startled blackbird's rage,
Caught on the cusp of day and night.

CONSIDERING ABSENCE

Gone is the breath between words that are lost
Here the tears. Here the wet. Here comes a frost

THE NUB

In the beginning, the up-springing
Before the tree, the acorn
Before the acorn
The acorn's kernel.

A MAN DIES TWICE

It is said,
A man dies twice
When he stops breathing
And when he is forgotten.

BIRDSONG

Birdsong, so much birdsong
A Belgium lace of notes
Tethered together, cross-stitched in harmony,
Hemmed and hung about the treetops.

By Brackfield Bawn

SHADOW I

Witness - river flow
Sun - climb and sink
Moon - wax and wane:

Those are shadows also
These, whose shadows
Come and go.

SHADOW II

Listen, the trees speak
A language older than ...
Sun or moon, earth or tree.

In the bleak beauty of these hills and this water
I am a shadow among shades
Dust between tree root and leafy bough.

SHADOW III

There would be no shadow
But for sun and for leaf
There would be no dance
But for wind and for leaf.

SHADOW DANCE I

River water runs, rain water falls
Beyond counting, toes and heels
Dance on the green sward.

A thousand leaves
A thousand shadows
Wind blown into a hundred harmonies.

SHADOW DANCE II

In the beginning, the seed; now
Buried at noon under shadow
Under earth and rock, the shadow's shadow grows.

Feeding worms ease themselves up and over
Forms of frugally well-knotted creation
Sap rises.

By Brackfield Bawn

THE QUICK AND THE DEAD

Homer knew a harpy named Podarge,
Light-footed, was she; gone now
Gone in a heartbeat, gone,
Gone, in the blink of an eye, gone
Though, when not deep in sleep's fastness
Fleet of foot was he, this our hero;
When winter sun fell in scuds, in scurries, so
Quick, quick as quicksilver, he hastened, he knew:
Time and tide wait for no man, so he,
He shot his speedy arrows to head and heart
The eagle, the skipping antelope, the hare
The quick child is soon taught he knew well
Glory is fleeting, but obscurity is forever
Turning, quick as a flash, he let it rip, having
Had till then, the time of his life, he continued
Living it up, life in the fast lane:

It came of course - the trip up, the crash;
In truth an epiphany, like a bolt of lightning.
In truth, he had not learned the requirements of speed.
Always a split second in front, he had failed
To consider the quick bee's thin sting,
To beware of the heavy bull's horned head.

Sam Burnside

BIRD CATCHERS

A wind comes in from the east, rattling through trees
Carrying clouds, their shadows blotting leaf-shadows
Tossing birds skywards, propelling them hither and thither.

By dawn's first light, closed doors swing open:
In their thousands they fly, knowing freedom
Testing their wings, all the while singing, singing.

Soon, the bird-catchers will be out and about
Up country lanes, on the streets of Belfast and Dublin,
Shutting fast all doors, wiring them tight, for ever.

By Brackfield Bawn

SAPPER JOHN

Buried deep and dark in his nest of blankets
Breathing in and out, in and out, he lies.
He swims in darkness, living other days.
Somewhere, a field gate swings shut.
A foot kicks: a booted foot pushes down on the spade's lug.
The horizon is a toe's length away.
His future is one narrow shadow, shortening.

THE CHOIR

There, across running water you can see the Donkey Field
While, high above greening leaves a skylark sings
Redeeming wounds inflicted and pain endured.

Beneath falling snow, a bugle sounds,
Striving to say so much.
The wee cuddy's ears twitch; bird and running water,
And bugle and beast: in such things,
The word peace is embodied.

By Brackfield Bawn

PARTING

Looking back, it was a sort of gift
Or was it merely a rift, a flaw in the day
The result of wind gusting, giving the morning a lift
Whatever it was, such a vista opened
And I saw clearly there, the road, the railway,
The winding river, (barged in blacks and blues)
Spread out, so crisply visible and so silent.
Before turning, I mouthed my last goodbye,
Waving, but not speaking, and in that moment
We understood the gesture sanctified.

TWELVE HUNDRED MOONS

And one by one in turn, some grand mistake
Casts off its bright skin yearly like the snake.
Lord Byron, *Don Juan, Canto V, Stanza 21*

1916
There -
A young woman walks
A flint road, brown cardboard suitcase
In one hand, her destination
Clutched in the other;
Called, as her grandmothers were,
To tend to the injured
The hurt and the dying
Her long coat, tight-fitted
Shadowing her innermost, her very deepest,
Clinch-fisted fears.
Now
She passes her brother's ditched plough
Light from stars skip off the dried dung
Stuck to its coulter.
That was the year the world changed
Stasis and movement, twin elements vying:
Meantime
Twelve hundred moons have come and gone
Since such poor people toed those
Twisting, ruinous, lying lines:
The Somme. The Post Office.
Insurrections. Risings.

Loyalties, allegiances and affections
And many little in-bred hatreds, also…
She journeys on
It is night and black clouded
She lilts one of her mother's old tunes.
Another grey dawn seeps across the sky
From over the hill, an explosion heralds another day
War will not end war

cont'd

Nor
Police states of the mind;
Nor, hip and breast and lip
Cocooned in old men's myths
Promoted by their self-ignited revulsion
The vanity of their beliefs roared, deafeningly.
Some lulls
Have been bought with flesh and blood.
Another war to end wars!
Now there's the rub...
2016
Above their heads stars glimmer, revealing
Rough-sleepers and junkies,
Their bodies no longer temples
But commodities, prostituted by rough weather
Remember
Shoulder to shoulder, as brothers might
Sisters too rise and march out
Supposing even as this new day breaks
Things can be altered, things will change.
Twelve hundred moons have passed
Since man and woman
First marked such doubtful lines.

NURSE

Working under canvas,
Against the cackle of gunfire
She thinks off and on of rainbows
Wiping stuff from her fingers
Looking out, remembering
Soft rain blowing in across distant Ulster fields, their smell,
Its washed trees, its mist-nourished hillsides.

She thinks now about rainbows,
Catching a reflection poised there
In the coolness of the white basin
Yearning for the feel of long grass about her ankles
Remembering, nettle stings on bare legs
Remembering, eggs, firm and fragile
Their hard-brittle warmth in her hands.

By Brackfield Bawn

WOMAN OF THE BOG

The thin rain falls. Flowers bow their heads.
The girl tucks up her skirts and steps across the peat bog
Ignoring the slopping glar, wading straight through
The water-logged peat, her footing all sponge. Floating so,
She gathers the sphagnum; with her two bared hands
She plucks and gathers the moss, her mind a dark pool.
The water is black as wet slate is,
It glows, as a dulled mirror might.
Straightening, she notices a billowy mass, reflected.
Momentarily, her armful of moss obscures the clouds
For that instant, she allows herself to remember:
She sees his drifting, shifting face.
She turns her back on the drenching slew.
She must think no more. She must be doing, bending, doing.

Sam Burnside

A BRACKFIELD YEAR

Spring
The light lengthens
The cold strengthens
Snowdrops' green-tipped spears appear
Nature's belly swells, new life draws near

Summer
Hold hands, hold hands, please let us all hold hands
For summer is come to us today
And whether we are going or whether we are coming, please,
Please hold hands
On this the merriest morning in May

Autumn
These slow mornings are mist inclined
Golden hoards stand solemn on the land
Men materialise, silver sickles to hand
The smell of baking bread drifts on the wind

Winter
A gale blows gusty and cold; the sun will be low;
We despair of this wolf-grey dawn's
Ever ending; summer has faded and is gone;
The day rests, still as a millpond;
Old men foretell the coming of snow

By Brackfield Bawn

FAUGHAN FIELD

The frosty field was white
Soot-black the birds
That hunkered there.

Peat-black and brackish
The river
Ice-honoured
With ribbon strung
If shyly so.

They spoke not once
Of Flanders's Field:
Bitter tongued
Hoarfrost bearded
Rime-eyed, they.

The field is white with frost
Soot-black and stiff the birds
That hunker here.

Sam Burnside

RHYTHM AND CLAY

Rain falls heavily from the sky
It falls on clay, it forms pools,
Sudden and shallow and pimpled.

The sound it makes is the sound of that last
Breath, the leaving sigh.

It takes to rivulets, to streams.
It leaves the clay veined and light-netted,
Riling; it moves to rivers, lakes, oceans.

The sound it makes is the silence of dreams,
The sounds of clouds being dreamt.

Water runs, sluices, flows, floods.
It splinters, hangs in smidgens, off trees,
Dripping sparkling diamond tiaras.

The sound it makes is the cascading of icicles
Shattering, breaking, splintering.

Rain drops in torrents from the sky:
The noise it makes is the slap, slap,
Slap of water striking water.

The sound carried is that of horses,
The pulse-beat on the air of close warm bodies fast approaching.

A gap opens: a rainbow emerges,
Revealing the sky's true colours, confiding
Where and how it buries its gold, carefully, slyly.

The sound it makes is the sound of a moth's wings:
A sail boat distant and alone, breasting the waves.

By Brackfield Bawn

THE UNBEGOTTEN

1914-1918

The gloaming settles down and there is time to think
Before battalions of what was once the future rise again
In answer to that phantom call.
From shadowy trenches they ascend, light as thistledown
In quick close-step, tight-lipped lads,
Again, and again and again, before they fall
Leaving no mark on grass or poppy-covered fields,
Leaving this behind. Leaving
Those ever-remembered soft empty arms of girls long missed.
The overwhelming sadness of all those children never to
Be kissed.
Descends. We might have avoided this. Perhaps,
But for the traps
Set by manhood's pride and for liberty's sake.
Who is to say,
That this vast dull emptiness was anyone's mistake.

Sam Burnside

STATES OF MIND

It was a madness
Called us
It was a madness
Carried us
In a black boat
On a cruel sea
To our ending:
Cliffs insurmountable
Our minster;
A cave
Our temple;
A grave
Our sanctuary;
This font
Of tears
Our cenotaph.

By Brackfield Bawn

OOR PLACE

It's a place o'
Bits a stane dykes
Wae nae clabber
Field stanes galore
Standin' in dry moul'
Laced together wae roots
Crowned by auld trees.

Topped by the Sperrins
Tailed by the Foyle
A quare auld bawn
On the one hand
The river Faughan
On the ither. Aye,
A settled place.

A giant lives here -
Not flesh and blood
But sap and seed -
A bold embodiment
Of those remembered dead
Upright here, ranked together,
Wae much solemnity.

Sam Burnside

THE NEW BRIDGE

Allowing that
History's chance and our customs did divide us
Let us now make good use of such a bridge:
Let us join the us and the other.

Forty thousand boards
Over running water, uniting failing fields,
Well-braced for peace, soundly-decked for friendship:
A hyphen to join us, not divide us.

By Brackfield Bawn

THE GREAT OAK TREE OF ARDMORE c. 1750

Follow me, into the Birch wood, among trees
To secret places, down hidden ways
To where the Faughan's onward flow is thwarted,
Turned, folded into serpentine coils.

Standing here, I hear from across
The years the haggard sound of a crosscut:
Before me I see my father and another,
Bent-backed, they find their rhythm
Their short pushes, their long pulls.

My old oak's frosty canopy shivers
Leaves now turned, become birds, fluttering,
Singing their long affair with this sacred place, there,
Dying leaves fall, like spectral snow, silently
Cold cobwebs tremble in chill dawn light
Insistent water buoys the air;
The musty smells of fusty mushrooms rise.

Whispered responses demand honour:
Here where passion's pulse works slow and easy
Under the ribbed canopy, green-laced and loose
Ghosts of old lovers and fretful penitents.
Pale initials glow beneath white snail-trails,
Ancient bark, ivy and briar garlanded.

To my eyes and ears, if not to my heart,
The mystery of this great sentient otherness -
This tree's destiny, to stand outside itself
A force obscure, impervious to the fleeting
Dreams, the nightmares of humanity.

This tree is aware of us: news carried by gales, cold and salty,
And by sand-weighted winds;
The very climate charged with news
Of wars and rumours of wars, intonations of blood and thunder
Seeping into sap, brought by rain and on air, bird carried,
Soul-to-body married.

Earth-bound memory-keeper
This monarch of time who has outstood each century
Of revolution and famine, seen them come and go.

We come, we go; the river flows.
The great Oak of Ardmore remains
The same, silent and sane.

By Brackfield Bawn

A STORM APPROACHES

8 November 2016

All morning the sky lowered while
Brackfield lay, as if under siege
Its inert, palsied trees skulking and brooding
In half-surrender. Until, at mid-afternoon,
The day seems to stir.
A breeze advances from the west
Having skimmed the Bluestacks
Whipping up and around the Sperrins
It twists between the Faughan's banks, intent
On brewing up a storm.
Out on the Foyle, something moves.
Another something sweeps in from the Swilly -
A gaudy of winds, greens and yellows, blacks and greys,
By-passing the Bogside, they move over Ardmore
Here to engage in this mad soiree.
Brackfield plays host to this commotion:
A gale tantalises the leafy tree-tops
The birds and the beasts have gone
Swept away by gusty squalls.
In an instant trees stir, nature trembles,
Branches break, the noise of their sudden cracklings
Smothered by this tempestuous hurricane.
Frisky offshoots play about tree roots.
Splinters dance, leaves dance, shovelled and spreading
The storm heaves big shadows up, to bop and hop,
Then casts them aside.
Being magically elastic, they spring back.
The air grows heavy, stupid, stiff, slow.
The woods float on a sea of shallow breaths, trees
Like patients, stand anaesthetised.

Sam Burnside

CODA

Brackfield Wood 1916-2016

That their deaths were not in vain
That is their legacy, rooted here
In branch and leaf endeared
Each tree equal, each the same.